When *Your Wife* has Tommy John Surgery

and other Baseball Stories

POEMS BY

E. ETHELBERT MILLER

City Point Press

City Point Press

PO Box 2063

Westport CT 06880

www.citypointpress.com

(203) 571-0781

Paperback ISBN: 978-1-947951-36-5

eBook ISBN: 978-1-947951-37-2

Printed in the United States

Cover design by Barbara Aronica-Buck

Cover photograph courtesy of Provident Hospital

Author photograph by Richard Harteis

This book is dedicated to my friends who love the game.

Jonathan Coleman

Mark Coleman

Jim Epstein

Aviva Kempner

Dan Moldea

Frazier O'Leary

Maria Otero

John Porter

Emily Rutter

Julie Walls

David Wilk

I never threw an illegal pitch. The trouble is, once in a while I toss
one that ain't never been seen by this generation.
–Satchel Paige

When they operated, I told them to put in a Koufax fastball.
They did – but it was Mrs. Koufax.
–Tommy John

Contents

Acknowledgments

It would have been impossible to write this book without my beloved friend and literary assistant Kirsten Porter.

Thanks once again to David Wilk for believing in my work.

Finally, special thanks to everyone who loves the game of baseball. Our lives are lived one pitch at a time.

Introduction

E. Ethelbert Miller is one of the most accomplished—if not *the* most accomplished—of contemporary baseball poets. This is one of many hats that Miller wears and perhaps this versatility is what makes his approach to baseball so richly layered and poignant. He begins this collection with two epigraphs by the iconic pitchers Satchel Paige and Tommy John (the latter of whom is also referenced in the collection's title). The coupling of these players and especially Paige's storied wit sets both the tone and the links between past and present that characterize the collection as a whole. Moreover, this collection works as a sequel of sorts to Miller's 2018 collection, *If God Invented Baseball*, which entangles the arc of the poet's lifetime with developments in baseball across the twentieth and twenty-first centuries. Similarly, in *When Your Wife Has Tommy John Surgery*, baseball is an evocative vehicle for documenting personal and sociocultural memories, including about the tumultuous present characterized by the COVID-19 pandemic, protests against anti-Black violence, and a watershed U.S. presidential election.

In Miller's skillful hands, baseball—a sport whose plays and rituals are irrevocably woven into the American vernacular—accrues new and layered significance. The autobiographical "Howard University, October 1969" recounts the camaraderie engendered by baseball for a young man "Still short on friends." When the 1969 New York Mets win the World Series, "I high five over the heads / of guys from Baltimore and Philly / All dazed / by the Amazin' Mets." This is just one of many moments in which baseball is a social lubricant and a common currency—a way of ordering human experience. The collection's title poem uses the metaphor of the surgery so many pitchers undergo to describe the fraying of intimacy in a marriage. Just as the arm is inexorably altered after a surgery in which a new tendon is grafted onto one's pitching elbow, so is a marriage when "You no longer recognize the rotation / of love, the spin of desire, the funny movement / of lust." It is fitting that this is the title poem, for it captures the brilliant combination of melancholy and humor that characterizes Miller's baseball verse more generally. If baseball is a way of explaining the world for Miller, the explanations are most often like the blues with the underlying impulse of resilience, or to laugh to keep from crying. As he notes in "The Swinging Sonnet Is Sung," "Baseball is a game of blues. You stand so you don't fall."

Unsurprisingly, Miller inflects his representations of Black baseball history with a similar blues mood. Satchel Paige and the many heroes of the Negro Leagues (1920–1960) dedicated their lives to a sport whose Major Leagues excluded them for decades. Put another way, Black baseball exemplifies making a way of no way, and what is more blues than that? Miller makes this analogy explicit in "The Negro League," when he writes about being in his office at Howard University:

I surrounded myself with the blues

and heavy hitters

Sterling Brown

Albert Murray

Richard Wright

Ralph Ellison

LeRoi Jones

and Josh Gibson

Notably, such a pantheon of Black blues writers concludes with the most accomplished of Negro League sluggers (Josh Gibson), affirming that the constellation of Black blues, baseball, and literary traditions work congruently to nourish and sustain Miller's poetic voice. Indeed, the final lines of this poem mimic Paige's own propensity for generating humorous maxims: "Control your love like Satchel Paige. / If you have to resuscitate then hesitate." Here and elsewhere, baseball and music are not only interwoven but also celebrated as crucial cultural and socio-political reference points for Black American life.

Invoking the title of Miles Davis's masterful album, Miller's poem "Kind of Blue" imagines a father who "watched the game while / Listening to Miles"; he stages a duet of sorts between "jazz / on the radio and the ball game / on television." These dual performances facilitate catharsis otherwise unavailable in a backbreaking job and an unforgiving city: "He worked / hard all week for life's tenderness." "In a Sentimental Mood" likewise compares the feeling evoked by Duke Ellington's famous composition to winning a high-stakes game and "savoring the moment" removed from celebrating teammates: "They are hugging and shouting. / I'm still looking at the field taking it all in." This is the poet both among and apart from the crowd, rendering timeless moments of joy and melancholy.

At times, baseball is an especially elegiac vehicle utilized to call attention to the systemic racism represented not only by the history of racial segregation that made the Negro Leagues necessary but also by the current era in which anti-Black discrimination and violence persist. In "Lost in the Sun," Miller paints this mournful picture:

> Black fathers no longer standing
> in a field of dreams
>
> Their Black boys gone
> sunglasses unable to hide their
>
> grief

Baseball has long been bound up in myths of American meritocracy—the field of dreams a potent image for unfettered opportunities. Miller punctures that illusion in his exposure of the oppressive forces beyond one's control that thwart the promises of youth and generational progress.

Similar attention to racial injustices and inequities characterizes "The Cardboard Season of 2020," which references the cutout fans placed in the seats of baseball stadiums to create the illusion of the crowds no longer deemed safe while a global pandemic spreads like wildfire. Summer 2020 was also, as Miller's first line announces, "The summer of Black Lives Matter," yet there remains a striking lack of Black agency in the predominantly white national pastime:

> we looked around the empty ball
> parks staring at Black cardboard
> faces—wondering who
> decided where to place us.

Bemoaning a more general sense of white control over Black lives—and, in the case of George Floyd, Ahmaud Arbery, Breonna Taylor, and so many others, Black deaths—Miller affirms that baseball (and sports more generally) is much more than a game. It reflects a nation riven with racial and intersectional disparities.

Alternatively, "The World Series" explains the stakes of contemporary life through a wide range (or series) of natural and human-made disasters. "One can go hitless and not understand poverty," the poem commences, and then continues with analogies to global warming, a hurricane, an earthquake, war, and finally concluding: "Every year the World Series is played with survivors." Reading this poem within the context of the 2020 season—one that will forever be asterisked because of the shortened and reconfigured schedule due to the COVID-19 pandemic—I'm struck by the word "survivor," suggestive of the multifold threats that we all face during this most trying and uncertain of times. As with Miller's baseball poetry more generally, "The World Series" is about much more than winning the game or the season at hand.

The poems in *When Your Wife Has Tommy John Surgery* also speak to Miller's virtuoso poetic skills, moving seamlessly between blues, jazz, confessional, persona, and ekphrastic modes without skipping a beat (or a base). Miller imagines conceptualist painter and sculptor Marcel Duchamp as "a manager / who can get away / with anything," Pablo Picasso in his Cubist phase seeing "the diamond as a cube, and, channeling Edward Hopper's *Nighthawks at the Diner*, the loneliness evoked by "The player whose girl / sits alone at the all-night / diner." While these poems are playful, they remind readers of the captivating visual symmetry of baseball, affirming that it stands alongside art, music, and poetry as a thing of beauty.

Baseball is not the cultural glue that it once was, with its fanbase older and whiter than the other two sports national pastimes: basketball and football. Despite these demographic and cultural realities, in Miller's poetry baseball is as relevant as ever, serving as both a window and mirror. With Miller's characteristic verve and wit, he offers a glimpse of what the game and, by extension, the nation could be while enjoining us to contemplate the ugly and beautiful aspects of our reflections. As he notes in the penultimate poem, "Just Let Us Play,"

Politicians try to be umpires.
They make and miss calls
outside the ballpark.
Let us play for the love
of the game.

Without naming the 45th president of the United States, Miller implies the devastation that he caused so many at home and abroad, and the poem implicitly champions the team-work and mutual respect required to play "for the love / of the game." As it has throughout this collection and much of Miller's oeuvre, baseball stands in for America, and this poem champions an inclusive ethos frequently lacking beyond the field. Miller thus concludes with a bilingual imperative: "Just let us play. *Juguemos.*"

In the collection's final poem—aptly titled "Extra Innings" — Miller moves into the interrogative mode, leaving readers to determine *how* and *why* we play this game of baseball (or life): "Is it for the love / of the game or the endless desire / for extra innings?" Put another way: What kind of player are *you*? These are the live questions that we must ask ourselves as we reckon with the inequities that structure our sports and, ultimately, our world. There is no better lyrical guide to the answers than the poems ahead.

Emily Ruth Rutter, Ph.D.
Associate Professor of English
Ball State University

When *Your Wife* has Tommy John *Surgery*

Hit This

Ball falling off table
curves.

Shortstop

People look at you
and can't determine your race.

You find yourself
between second and third.

Oh, how beautiful you are
flipping in the air like Ozzie
Smith.

Girl in a Ball Park with Her Back to the Stands

for Julie

I was the best player
on my block, in my neighborhood,
in my school.

I could
run, hit
and catch.

I guess it's because of catching
I'm sitting by the foul line
in right field.

I chase after foul balls
then flip them to those boys
in the stands with open gloves.

People probably wonder why
I'm not wearing a dress
or singing in the church choir.

Roberto

Some kids in the projects
didn't have gloves. They caught better
barehanded or so they wanted us to believe.

Roberto's mother got him Converse
sneakers but they had no star in the logo.
He cried until we left him alone.

It was all his mother could afford.
We didn't know this because we were
children and had no kids of our own.

We had gloves. Cheap gloves. Gloves
with no pockets no matter how much
we kept punching into the center of them.

The gloves had missing pockets
like our missing fathers who punched
our mothers and swung bats at our heads.

Our fathers were gone and we outgrew their
absence. Our hands became too large
for small gloves. Many were lost or stolen.

One winter we threw and caught snowballs
with stiff fingers. Roberto once got me good and
kept laughing saying he was "Clemente."

That was the year after he discovered
he was Puerto Rican and Spanish
had yet to melt in his mouth.

Whitey Ford

Growing up I was seen as odd
not because of height or weight but because
I was left-handed.

My mother placed a fork in my right hand
a pencil too. It was the 1950s and everyone
was called colored.

On the playground I played baseball.
Kids teased me because of my fair skin.
They called me "Whitey Ford."

It was the Black catcher Elston Howard
who nicknamed Ford "the chairman of the board."
It was my father who taught me how to fight back.

He taught me how to take care of business.

Third Base

I didn't move when the ball shot into left field.
It reminded me of the time I was robbed in the Bronx.
A guy pulled a gun and I froze.
He said I was too close to his manhood, his space,
his third base line.
I had walked into a strange neighborhood
where they spoke a Blackness I didn't understand.

The Batting Order

Everyone knows you can't hit
so you're the last kid picked.

You can't dance so you're
always against a wall.

God places dice in your hands.
You forget he's a gambler.

Like Adam you're the leadoff hitter.
Eve is batting second.

The Night Before September 29, 1954

The ball was hit to the deepest
part of sleep. I caught it the night before.
I ran with my back to the infield.
Everyone saw the number 24 on my back.
The catch was not a miracle.
I was Black and a Giant.

The ball dropped into my basket.
Turning like a dervish I threw it
to second base. Wertz was wordless.
The fans in the Polo Grounds went crazy
as I rose from my dream.

—

May 28, 1957

Brooklyn broke down when the Bums
left. Hearts died in Flatbush.
Ebbets Field silent. When I mentioned
Duke to a fool in Harlem he thought
I was talking about Ellington.

Howard University, October 1969

Cook Hall. A dark basement
rec room. A pool table and television.

I'm a sophomore growing an afro.
Still short on friends.

But now I high five over the heads
of guys from Baltimore and Philly.

All dazed
by the Amazin' Mets.

I hide my South Bronx accent
and say I'm from Brooklyn -

well this time Queens. I love baseball
miracles more than a college degree.

Ornette

When you reach second base
you feel like Ornette Coleman
standing on a stage in Texas.
Alone. A new music blowing
in from centerfield. You felt
something different when the bat
hit the ball. Your fingers racing
past first, ears yet to be fans.

Kind of Blue

The father was always somewhere
in the back of the house with jazz
on the radio and the ball game
on television. The small space
in the house was his space. He worked
hard all week for life's tenderness.

The father watched the game while
listening to Miles. A player swung
and sent a fly ball toward the outfield
fence. It went foul at the last moment
like love or a marriage striking an
empty wooden seat and bouncing
back to the field.

So what.

The Scout

There are times
when I feel Edward Hopper
looking over my shoulder
staring at stats.

Everything in front of me
and sometimes nothing there.
I stare at my laptop
the only light in the room.

Every kid's dream a daydream.
I shadow players looking
for the one who plays ball
until it's dark outside.

The player whose girl
sits alone at the all-night
diner.

Manager Descending Down the Batting Order

Who should hit first?
Who should bat second?
What determines order?

A good pitcher will find
a lineup hole like found art
in an alley.

Marcel Duchamp
is a manager
who can get away

with anything.

The Rundown

It's always the abstract expressionist
who gets caught.

How do you explain
that?

Picasso

Picasso attends his first
baseball game and sees
the diamond as a cube.

Hamiltonian Artists

for Angie Goerner

Grace and I are walking on U
Street. It's October. Leaves
are falling and they will miss you
as much as I do.

Yesterday the Nats lost another
playoff game. Rick sent an email
at 2 am. He lost track of the pitch
count.

There is no beauty left in life
when it breaks your heart every
10th month. Angie can you see us
crying?

There are no paintings on the gallery
walls. The Hamiltonian
was closed today. Life imitating
art.

The World Series

One can go hitless and not understand poverty.

A shutout has nothing to do with income inequality.

A wild pitch might be a hurricane.

An earthquake is when the bullpen collapses.

Global warming is a manager pacing in a dugout.

War is when players race across the field to throw punches and not pitches.

Every year the World Series is played with survivors.

Don Larsen for a Day
(October 8, 1956)

Man is not perfect

Man makes errors.

Did God ever make a mistake?

If only one could be Don Larsen for a day.

Who wouldn't want Yogi Berra to leap into their arms?

In a Sentimental Mood

When Ellington plays those first
notes my back is against the dugout wall.
I'm alone savoring the moment.
My teammates in the clubhouse
going crazy with champagne.
They are hugging and shouting.
I'm still looking at the field taking it all in.

The Called Third Strike

When you first saw her she was a red light
in the corner of your eye. You watched how
she walked, how she sat, how she spoke
and all the time you said nothing. Your legs
froze and then your arms and then you
turned your head away knowing the moment
was over and she would never notice you.

The Unexpected

You never know when
you're in the batter's box
and a lover tries to steal
home.

When Your Wife Has Tommy John Surgery

Your wife says you need therapy.
Her words keep hitting the corner of the plate.
You step out of the box and talk to yourself.
You already know the next pitch that's coming.

It's the argument that leaves her hands
with marriage deception. It's the hard fast
stuff, the slamming of a door, the turning
of the back in bed.

You can no longer recognize the rotation
of love, the spin of desire, the funny movement
of lust. Your wife has changed and now she's
seeing someone else.

The Designated Hitter

All your life you've been in the wrong
league. You hold your head in your hands
every evening at the dinner table. You
live a life of hunger and despair.

While everyone is romancing the field
you find yourself in the dugout holding
a bat, wanting to hit yourself in the head.

Some folks say you wouldn't know
the difference between a glove and love.

Free Agent

There is the silence between phone calls
that soon becomes equal to the distance
between bases or the mound to the plate.

The first sounds of spring come from your
muscles, followed by the sound of fingers
now fists punching into gloves.

You want someone to remember your youth
before night comes or the sky with the wind's
farewell, the darkened scoreboard.

The empty bleachers.

Domestic Violence

Why is everyone surprised
when the bat breaks
in my hands?

In Between Innings

"He's upstairs doin' nothin or probably
watchin' that stupid game if not that
then just sittin' in the dark."

I hear her voice like the smell of chitlins
cookin' on the stove. It's a passed ball.
Something I can't forget.

For Love of the Game

After the 4th walk I turn the television off.
I know we will have to move again.
John is going back to the minors.
What was once his dream was now something
I wanted to close my eyes to. It was getting hard
to sleep next to him.

There are nights when I can no longer rub his arm.
His arm keeps a roof over our heads. His arm is hurting
and he knows there are few chances left. I married
the man I love. A man who once had control
of his pitches and his life. I pray when he comes
home tonight he won't walk away from me.

Pitching Is No Way to Treat a Muse

After the shower
he sits on the bed like he was in the bullpen.
I gently touch the scoreboard of his back.
I've been with him since the first inning
of high school. The ups and downs like
our love making. I was his second dream.
The first was baseball. I was his mistress
and muse. I was often like a manager
who took the ball from the starting pitcher
waiting for the reliever to arrive. My girlfriend
said there is always another woman warming
up. Why does baseball have such beautiful
legs?

The No-Hitter

Around the 6th inning
I start feeling like I'm flirting
with my first wife again.

I hold the ball in my hand
thinking of hers. I once
inhaled her scent like it was
a hard grounder to third.

Then there is the loneliness
I felt when she left and I know
I have to get three last outs.

Nothing more. Nothing less.

The Blown Save

You scream at the screen
until your yelling tells you
to shut up and sit down.
It's disbelief you're watching.

9th inning and no trumpets
for your team, no more take
me out to the ball game.

Your team is no longer leading
not even tied, but down by two.
Your third beer is warm, the taste
of defeat swimming down
your throat.

You keep remembering the factory
layoff, the pink slip, the unpaid bills.
This is not the life you wanted.
Your savings are blown.

You're not a closer today.
But memory is short and you're
gonna play with your kids
tomorrow.

Mudcat

Before there was Mookie Wilson
or Mookie Betts there was Mudcat
Grant in Minnesota and before that
Ohio. Someone thought Mudcat
was from Mississippi but he was from
Lacoochee, Florida, a lumber town.

Mudcat was a pitcher who could hit.
Some teams believed colored players
couldn't swim in the ocean.
Mudcat was saved by the big fisherman
Larry Doby. Doby taught Mudcat the ways
of fresh water.

The Negro League

I worked 40 years at Howard.
Mule could have done more.

Everything in my office was second-hand.
I safe surrounded myself with the blues
and heavy hitters:

Sterling Brown
Albert Murray
Richard Wright
Ralph Ellison
LeRoi Jones
and Josh Gibson

One afternoon after lunch
I sold my soul near the Sundial.

I was Cool Papa Bell before
the sun came out.

They said I hit like Robert Johnson
but ran like B.B. King.

When I was a student
Ma Rainey tried to take me home
which is why I never left.

Don't let a blueswoman touch
the back of your head. Don't let her
hear your Howlin' Wolf.

Control your love like Satchel Paige.
If you have to resuscitate then hesitate.

The Third Base Coach

I know everyone doesn't trust me.

When they see my Black hands
telling them to stop or slide
they keep running.

My job isn't easy. How many
Black third base coaches do you
see in the sporting news?

I'm the invisible man when
it comes to hiring managers.
I'm the kid with the cotton
candy on his face.

What sticks is the racism
and the foul balls hit behind
my butt. What's lost is
my sweet taste for the game.

Lost in the Sun

Joyful Black fathers
throwing their little ones into the air

Years later a troubling blue sky
blankets the world

Black fathers at funerals
no longer able to catch their sons

Black fathers no longer standing
in a field of dreams

Their Black boys gone
sunglasses unable to hide their

grief

Stolen Secrets from the Ground Crew

When I lift the bags from the field
no one suspects I wanted to be Ty
Cobb, Maury Wills, Lou Brock
or Rickey Henderson. I know more
about basepaths than anyone.
I drive the bank robbers to the bank.

The Cardboard Season of 2020

The summer of Black Lives Matter
we looked around the empty ball
parks staring at Black cardboard
faces - wondering who
decided where to place us.

True Confessions of a Baseball

1.

If they would replace my stitches
with cornrows I'm certain I could
attract more Black pitchers.

2.

When you come from a large family
people will toss you back and forth.

3.

People keep falling over seats for me.
Who needs a rain delay with so much
seduction in the air?

4.

I tell folks I have to always be handled
with gloves.

5.

Every time I brush against a man's
jersey he tries to get to first base.

The Beanball

You didn't see the election coming.

You tried to duck but it was too late.
You mistook a curve for a fastball.

As you lie on the ground
both dugouts empty -

Your helmet continues to spin
like a country out of control.

Conversations with My Body

for Leslie

My body is snoring
keeping me awake
so I don't die in my sleep.

The night is more peaceful
than the day. Yesterday I
learned another friend

was dying. A slow death.
The kind you encounter
when you turn the pages

of a newspaper and a celebrity
you knew by face and name
died and now you know their

age. They are either younger
or older than you. This provides
a sense of comfort, a knowing

that people your age are still
alive. What bothers me at times
are the baseball players

whose baseball cards I once
held in my young hands. Hands
covered with sugar dust

from bubblegum. How long
will I live and will I live longer
than the longest game?

My friends are now in hospices.
The place where the umpires
turn their backs and remove

their masks. Leaving the
field they walk with
heads bowed while you

stand in the batter's box
pondering the third strike
before returning to the

dugout to face not an
understanding manager
but the face of God.

A Rookie During the Season of Coronavirus

Eight years in the minors.
Today my rookie season begins
with only shadows in the ballpark.

No cheers or boos.
Just the silent green in front of me
as if this was a high school field trip.

After the swollen fingers, bruised thighs
and disappointments I need more than
this.

I need to give someone my autograph,
throw balls into the stands and smile
at a fan hanging over the dugout rail.

How can something end before it begins?
I thought baseball was forever.

After the Swinging Sonnet Is Sung

The 7th Inning finds you no longer playing the numbers.
Your body is growing old. When you stand you sing
"take me out to the funeral home, I don't care if I ever
come back." Your pants covered with peanut dust. Your shirt
with mustard from the second inning. The game was once
slow. A pitcher's battle. Hits were hard to come by. Your
first wife was left on second. Your second wife
never got to third. Life is a lonely game. The dugout
is the only home you've ever known but lately you've
become a spectator with a crowd. You're a fan on a hot day.
Baseball is a game of blues. You stand so you don't fall.
It's time to stretch but you're reaching too far. It was
the Devil who promised extra innings. God said
"pray for a rally and you might see the 9th."

Tommy John Knocks on the Bedroom Door

1.

Once my arm around her
was like circling the bases.
She was the woman I came home to.

Now my arm talks
in its sleep. The pain throbbing
here and there. My wife sleeps
in another room.

2.

They call him a Bionic Man.
His arm repaired as if someone
had taken him to Mr. Thompson's auto repair
on the corner.

3.

He might never pitch again. His elbow gone. Blown.
What is *ulnar collateral ligament reconstruction*?
Where did they take the tendon from?

Tommy John was an All-Star in 1968.
So many died that year. MLK and RFK.
Tommy John was on the mound one day in 1974.
That day the butcher came and cut him down.

Grown men are known to cry when led from the field.
Their arms limp. A manager's hand on their shoulders.
Dreams die when they reach that first step of the dugout.

4.
The TJS Team:
Paul Molitor
John Smoltz
Jamie Moyer
Pedro Borbon
Joba Chamberlain
Patrick Corbin
Johnny Cueto
Travis d'Arnaud
Yu Darvish
Didi Gregorius
Matt Harvey
Tim Hudson
Spencer Kieboom
Charlie Morton
Shohei Ohtani
Chris Sale
Drew Storen
Stephen Strasburg
Noah Syndergaard
Justin Verlander
Adam Wainwright
Zack Wheeler
Jordan Zimmermann

Baseball's Trinity

Hitter
Catcher
Umpire

Standing at the
crossroads
of home plate

Watching a ball
rise to
heaven

The Closer

You need three outs.
You stand on the mound
nodding to your therapist.

Nothing seems to be working.
You can't find the plate but it doesn't
matter.

A closer has a short memory.
You hold the ball in your hand.
Nothing feels round tonight.

Just Let Us Play

From Puerto Rico and Cuba
to the Dominican Republic.
From South Korea to Japan.

We play the game we love.
We marry bats, balls and gloves.

We create diamonds in alleys
or find them in open fields.

Politicians try to be umpires.
They make and miss calls
outside the ballpark.

Let us play for the love
of the game.

Just let us play. *Juguemos*

Extra Innings

The new rule places a man on second base
at the beginning of the 10th inning.
This is another example of privilege.
If you had been born rich you found
yourself on third. How did you get there?
What baseball scandal cheated you to this
place? What if God wanted to speed up
the game? What if you were born in your
grave? What sacrifice would have to be
made in order for you to live? Why do
you want to live? Is it for the love
of the game or the endless desire
for extra innings?

When the Games Return
(for Emily)

When the games return
we will not hide behind the mask.
We will race out onto the field
to bask in fellowship and embrace
the sky, sun, and the four bases below.

There will be no fear in the air,
no sickness in the stands. There
will only be cheering and clapping
and a knowing that baseball is what
matters and our dreams are round
and hard and at times get caught
in our gloves.

When the tarp is lifted and rolled
back a sudden beauty will appear.
It will be the memories of what
we missed and what we love. It will
be baseball. It will be prayer.

About the Author

E. Ethelbert Miller is a writer and literary activist. He is the author of two memoirs and several books of poetry including *The Collected Poems of E. Ethelbert Miller,* a comprehensive collection that represents over 40 years of his work. For 17 years Miller served as the editor of *Poet Lore,* the oldest poetry magazine published in the United States. His poetry has been translated into nearly a dozen languages. Miller is a two-time Fulbright Senior Specialist Program Fellow to Israel. He holds an honorary degree of Doctor of Literature from Emory and Henry College and has taught at several universities.

Miller is host of the weekly WPFW morning radio show *On the Margin with E. Ethelbert Miller* and host and producer of *The Scholars* on UDC-TV which received a 2020 Telly Award. In recent years, Miller has been inducted into the 2015 Washington DC Hall of Fame and awarded the 2016 AWP George Garrett Award for *Outstanding Community Service in Literature* and the 2016 DC Mayor's Arts Award for *Distinguished Honor*. In 2018, he was inducted into Gamma Xi Phi and appointed as an ambassador for the Authors Guild. Most recently, Miller was given a grant by the D.C. Commission on the Arts and Humanities and a congressional award from Congressman Jamie Raskin in recognition of his literary activism. Miller serves on the boards of the DC Collaborative for Humanities and Education and *The Inner Loop*. His first book of baseball poems *If God Invented Baseball*, published by City Point Press, was awarded the 2019 Literary Award for poetry by the Black Caucus of the American Library Association. Miller's forthcoming book is a haiku collection entitled *the little book of e*.